GW00401821

KAKAPO
COUNTRY

This book is dedicated to the memory of
Clarence Cemmick
and to all who provide support for
those working to save the kakapo from extinction

By the same artist and author
BLACK ROBIN COUNTRY

KAKAPO COUNTRY

THE STORY OF THE
WORLD'S MOST UNUSUAL BIRD

DAVID CEMMICK
&
DICK VEITCH

HODDER AND STOUGHTON
AUCKLAND LONDON SYDNEY TORONTO

Copyright © 1987 David Cemmick and Dick Veitch
First published 1987
ISBN 0 340 424850

All rights reserved. No part of this publication may be reproduced or transmitted in any form or by any means, electronic or mechanical, including photocopy, recording, or any information storage and retrieval system, without permission in writing from the publisher.

Typeset by Glenfield Graphics Ltd, Auckland.
Printed and bound in Hong Kong for Hodder & Stoughton Ltd, 46 View Road, Glenfield, Auckland, New Zealand.

Contents

A rock wren carrying a kakapo feather to its nest.

Foreword

Do you want your children to grow up in a world of sheep walks, paddocks and pine trees — a world devoid of natural interest and stripped of all but those species of plants and animals which are of direct utilitarian value? If not, read on.

Kakapo Country is the story of New Zealand's rarest and most unusual bird — the kakapo — and of the desperate attempt to save it from extinction. The kakapo is a parrot unlike any other in the world. It cannot fly, walks abroad only at night, booms like a bittern, displays like a grouse and, like the latter bird, can accurately 'predict' how plentiful the next crops of its chosen food plants will be.

Once, the kakapo was widespread throughout New Zealand, its home the dark recesses of the native forest where it had evolved a nocturnal lifestyle to avoid its few natural enemies. As a result of habitat modification that accompanied human settlement and predation by and competition for food from introduced animals, there are today only 50 kakapo known to be surviving — it is a population in critical decline, beleaguered by rats, cats and possums.

Ironically, the only real hope for the survival of this unique species rests with man. But for the care and hard work of a band of dedicated people, *Strigops habroptilus* — the kakapo — would be no more, extinct like the moa which once shared its habitat.

For a number of years, field workers have been locating the few kakapo that remain in the wild, finding out as much as possible about the birds and their requirements and moving those that are endangered to predator-free forests. And the work continues. The story of this project, recorded here, is one of struggle and immense dedication, and of much finger crossing, for, as knowledge of this secretive, nocturnal species is difficult to obtain and as the bird's predators still exist, each move by field workers to save the kakapo contains an element of risk.

Kakapo Country is a classic story of conservation, one that highlights nature's delicate balance and provides an inspiration to work with, not against, the natural world. Illustrated with David Cemmick's wonderful artwork, that also depicts many other of New Zealand's native species, it is a book that will give the reader much pleasure as well as an appreciation of the variety of New Zealand's wildlife.

Thank you for caring.

David Bellamy
Bedburn, 1987.

Tui

Author's Note

To begin my career in conservation with the New Zealand Wildlife Service (now part of the Department of Conservation) it was necessary for me to work for almost a year as a clerical cadet. Weekends, however, were spent helping with any wildlife field project near at hand. One such visit, in 1961, was to the newly constructed Mount Bruce Native Bird Reserve (now the National Wildlife Centre), near Masterton, where I met 'Bashful', the first live kakapo I had seen but the last survivor of five kakapo caught in Fiordland in 1959. He did not look handsome or interesting as he sat in hiding during the day and we could not see what he did by night. At that time public interest in active conservation was low and technology to study nocturnal birds virtually absent. Although it was understood that the kakapo population had become smaller and the bird's range was restricted to only a few areas, too little was known of the habits or true status of the wild kakapo for there to be major interest in this unusual species or for us to need to make major conservation efforts.

When the status of the kakapo was recognised as being close to perilous, however, work by the Wildlife Service to save the species from extinction increased. At irregular intervals during the 1960s and '70s, I worked in kakapo country, searched for and found kakapo sign, marvelled at the grandeur of the forests and mountains where the birds now live, and sorrowed at the prospect of the species' almost sure demise, wondering what we could do to prevent it. It was almost 20 years before I saw a kakapo in the wild.

Many field trips have followed to search for more birds, study them and their habitats. Now the plight of the relatives of Bashful is much more apparent and we also have some means to help them.

When David Cemmick joined me in 1984 for the field work for a book about New Zealand's most endangered bird, the black robin — *Black Robin Country* — we naturally discussed the kakapo, at that time the second most endangered bird in New Zealand. We then visited Fiordland, the mainland's last significant kakapo habitat, and decided that, should *Black Robin Country* be successful, we would work together on a book about the kakapo.

David Cemmick has always been fascinated by the natural world. For several years the focus of his work as an artist was the portrayal of the colour, detail and diversity of nature. He would spend many hours just observing wildlife in natural environments and making annotated sketches which were later used to produce detailed portraits in the comfort of a studio.

After some time David realised that the simple sketches were his real interest and that further studio work was a less stimulating continuation. An economical, well-observed sketch can bring life and movement to a subject which extra detail tends to destroy. So David's aims changed. Instead of waiting for the subjects to stay still before sketching, he sought to capture the quick actions of preening, feeding and movement. He found that these rapid sketches of behavioural attitudes and habits helped to explain the complex requirements each species has for life.

To produce the artwork for *Kakapo Country*, David joined Wildlife Service expeditions to Stewart Island, Fiordland and Little Barrier Island to study and sketch kakapo, their present habitats and species which share the forest with the kakapo.

The kakapo is now the rarest bird in New Zealand and very few New Zealanders are ever likely to see a live bird, let alone actively assist in its conservation. The inspiration for *Kakapo Country* came from these two facts and from the urgent need to help protect what remains of New Zealand's wildlife.

Dick Veitch
Auckland, 1987

Artist's Note

It has been a joy and a privilege to work with such a remarkable bird as the kakapo. As an artist I feel it is my duty to observe and paint from life as this is the only way of portraying the vitality which is so important to an animal's survival.

During my travels I have seen and drawn many wonderful creatures but never before have I felt such a deep involvement with a subject as I have whilst working with the kakapo. It is a species for which I developed a deep respect and affection.

The artwork produced for *Kakapo Country* includes portraits and sketches of many other species still to be found in New Zealand's more remote areas.

I sincerely hope that in years to come this book will be seen not as the last records in the kakapo story, but as a celebration of a turning-point in the history of a bird no longer threatened with extinction, and a tribute to some of New Zealand's unique wildlife and natural beauty.

David Cemmick
North Yorkshire, 1987

Acknowledgements

Preparation of this book has given David Cemmick and myself a unique opportunity to work alongside scientists and field workers in their studies of the problems of conservation and management of endangered species. The difficulties experienced and the many political and financial hurdles to be faced in the pursuit of conservation goals are recognised by too few people. The dedication of New Zealand conservationists, their generosity of spirit, genuine concern for the species they are dealing with and single-mindedness in their objectives must be acknowledged and appreciated.

We are indebted to the following organisations and individuals who provided financial sponsorship and support for David's visit to New Zealand: The Peter Nathan Cultural Trust, the Augustine Trust, the Robinson Charitable Trust, Northern Arts, Barclays Bank PLC, Whessoe PLC, Darlington Borough Council, Ian Armstrong of the Royal Society for the Protection of Birds, Julie Gaman of the Durham County Conservation Trust, Peter Robinson of Thomas Watson and Son, the Peoples Trust for Endangered Species, Windsor and Newton (for the supply of art materials), Mr and Mrs Richard Brown, Mr R. Brown, Mr and Mrs M. Burton, the Reverend Canon and Mrs P.B. Carter, Mrs M.D. Cemmick, Mr and Mrs C. Denton, Mr and Mrs G.W. Forbes, Mrs J. Gardner, Mr D.Q. Gurney, Mr and Mrs I.D. Hunter, Mr and Mrs Richard Lawson, Mr and Mrs D. Luckhurst, Mr and Mrs Miller, Mr and Mrs D.A. and V. Oliver, Mr and Mrs P. Richardson, Mr and Mrs R. Sellars, Mr and Mrs L. Taylor, Mr and Mrs B. Verdon, Mr and Mrs E.F. and A. Welding.

While I remained at home working on the text, David travelled to kakapo country and received unequalled hospitality from friends as well as people neither of us had met before. We are most grateful for their time, patience and assistance, for without their help this book would not have been possible. Particular thanks are due to Lynn Harris of the New Zealand Wildlife Service; Ian Bryant and the staff of the National Wildlife Centre, Mt Bruce; Eric Fox and the staff of the Otorohanga Kiwi House; and to Dick Anderson, Craig Batchelor, Mike and Alex Dobbins, Chris Challis, Dave Crouchley, Andy Cox, Graeme Elliott, Bernard and Connie Goetz, Ian McLean, Rod and Julia Morris, Ron Nilsson, Peter Reese, Bruce Thomas, Jack van Berkel, Arnie and Connie Wright.

Special thanks are due to Don Merton, Rod Morris and Ralph Powlesland for their excellent advice and help during the preparation of the manuscript.

Last, but far from least, our very sincere thanks to Elizabeth and Bryony who support us in this work.

Introduction

When the land mass that became New Zealand separated from the ancient southern supercontinent of Gondwanaland more than 60 million years ago, it was early enough in the evolution of animal life forms for the ancestors of some species to be already present. Among these were large flightless birds — the kiwi and the moa; a diminutive relative of the dinosaurs — the tuatara; and some insects. But there were no terrestrial mammals — none had yet arrived in the Australian region, the land from which ancient New Zealand parted. The ancestors of all other native birds, insects and lizards, and New Zealand's only native land mammals — two species of bat — reached New Zealand by sea or air. Because of the land's early isolation, most of its wildlife was avian.

Among the earlier of the post-Gondwanaland arrivals must have been the kakapo, or its ancestors, a large owl-like parrot that was to become one of New Zealand's unique species, found nowhere else in the world.

Flightless and nocturnal now but in earlier times the kakapo could probably fly and perhaps wandered about in the daylight too. From fossil evidence it is known that the kakapo, more or less as it is today, was certainly in New Zealand 15,000 years ago. There are no obvious reasons for the bird to have become heavy, flightless and nocturnal, only that long ago, with no predators present, there was probably no need to fly and to avoid predatory birds it may have been very convenient to become nocturnal. Or perhaps the kakapo became nocturnal and then found it was unsafe to fly at night.

Just how the kakapo's unusual breeding system evolved is also a mystery. It differs from the breeding systems of all other parrots and is more akin to the breeding patterns of some species of grouse, the cotinga, hermit hummingbird and a few other species.

In the totally forested New Zealand before the arrival of man, the kakapo, like many other species, was widespread. As a consequence of human settlement, however, first by Polynesians, from about AD 800, then by Europeans, from the early nineteenth century, kakapo numbers, amongst others, began to decline rapidly. Directly or indirectly, man destroyed their habitats and deliberately or by accident introduced predatory animals. These changes to the land were the primary cause of the extinction of 17 native bird species, but the kakapo survived, albeit precariously.

As early as 1840 explorers and ornithologists had observed, commented on and tried to remedy the decline of the kakapo. More recently, from the late 1950s, staff of the New Zealand Wildlife Service (now part of the Department of Conservation) have been working to learn about the kakapo in order to save it from extinction. For the species to survive, its habitats need to be predator-free or new secure habitats have to be found, and the right food must be available for breeding to be successful.

In total, hundreds of people from all walks of life have helped with this work, paid and unpaid, in the field and behind the scenes, from newly appointed clerk to cabinet minister, and still the work continues. With so many people involved over so many years it is not possible to include their names here, or even mention the work that many have done.

Today, with a total known population of just 50 birds, the kakapo is New Zealand's most critically endangered bird.

People have been watching all kinds of birds for hundreds of years. About some we know a lot and about most we know a little. The kakapo, however, being noctural, cryptically coloured, very rare, very secretive, living in remote parts and not breeding every year, is extremely difficult to observe. By putting all the available observations together, however, and adding a little supposition, we now do know a great deal about the kakapo and are using this information to try to save this remarkable species.

Kakapo Country is primarily the story of the kakapo, its habits and habitats, and the efforts of conservationists to help the species survive. It is also an informal pictorial study of other inhabitants of kakapo country — native plants, small animals and birds which enhance wild New Zealand with their colour and variety, and it is a record of the environmental damage wrought by man and his introduced animals.

Black Petrel *Procellaria parkinsoni*
The black petrel is a migratory species, coming to New Zealand each spring from
its winter home in the eastern tropical Pacific. Because of predation by cats and stoats,
breeding populations of this once widespread species are now found only on Great
Barrier and Little Barrier islands.

Opposite
Tuatara *Sphenodon punctatus*
Often called a 'living fossil', the lizard-like tuatara, unique to New Zealand, is one
of the most primitive of living reptiles. It once occurred in coastal forests throughout
the country, but is now restricted to about 30 offshore islands. The tuatara is
carnivorous, feeding mainly on insects, but is also known to eat small lizards and
the eggs and chicks of seabirds.

A Most Unusual Bird

The kakapo (*Strigops habroptilus*) is a unique bird, a parrot unlike any other in the world and it is found only in New Zealand. It is flightless, nocturnal and solitary and has a breeding system otherwise unknown in its avian order.

Only by attaching small transmitters to selected birds to track their movements and by watching through special night-vision scopes, have we been able to learn about the kakapo and its activities.

While the kakapo cannot fly it does have wings and some writers have described a 'gliding flight', but the best that the bird can achieve is a controlled free-fall — a child's handkerchief parachute is a better flier. The male kakapo, however, does use his wings at breeding time as part of a display to attract a female. Although flightless, the kakapo is nonetheless not restricted to the ground; it can climb trees very skilfully — to get food it is very necessary for it to be able to do so. And on its sturdy legs the kakapo can walk long distances. When observed moving about in its home range the bird appears to wander haphazardly in an unhurried manner but it can cover many kilometres in one night as it searches for food.

All the kakapo's feeding, as well as breeding and other activities, take place at night. The birds sleep during the day, usually in a sheltered spot, although occasionally they may seek a warm place in the sun.

By day and by night their mottled moss- or olive-green plumage, which is similar in both sexes, blends well with the natural forest vegetation but in some lights the feathers display iridescent edges.

The kakapo is a large bird, unusual particularly for its weight. With the male measuring some 60 centimetres from head to toe and weighing up to three kilograms, the kakapo is by weight the largest parrot in the world. The female is a little lighter in weight but not much different in length. The most obvious differences between the sexes are the narrower face and bill of the female.

Two particularly unusual facial features which the kakapo has evolved are an owl-like facial disc, to help the bird see at night, and cat-like whiskers, to assist with its feeding. These are not features commonly associated with a parrot.

It is generally assumed that larger birds live longer than smaller birds but once a bird attains its adult plumage there is no way of ascertaining the age of that bird unless it is somehow marked for identification. We have not been studying the kakapo for long enough and too few chicks have been produced for us to know how old a bird might be before it breeds or for how long it might live.

The breeding system of the kakapo, unique amongst parrots, is shared by

RECENT AND CURRENT HOMES OF THE KAKAPO

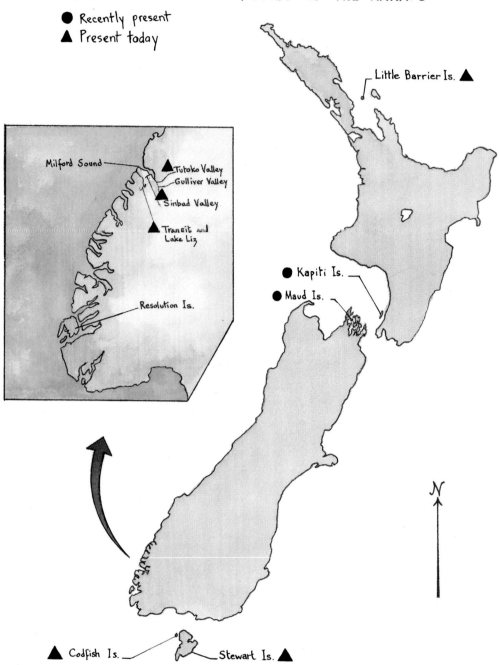

● Recently present
▲ Present today

Little Barrier Is. ▲

Milford Sound ▲ Tutoko Valley
Gulliver Valley
▲ Sinbad Valley
▲ Transit and Lake Liz

Resolution Is.

● Kapiti Is.
● Maud Is.

N

▲ Codfish Is. Stewart Is. ▲

Kakapo originally occurred throughout New Zealand. This map shows places referred to in the text – areas where the kakapo are present today as well as some of the areas where birds were recently present or transferred to. Codfish, Maud, Kapiti and Little Barrier islands are reserves and public access is prohibited. Visits to these islands may be made only with authorisation from the Department of Conservation. Resolution Island, where transferred kakapo existed until about 1908, is still a reserve and part of Fiordland National Park.

18

only a few other bird and animal species. Known as lek breeding, it is a system whereby in the breeding season the males congregate in one area, make booming noises to inform the females and one another that they are there, then compete, by displays and calls, for the favours of females. Hence the kakapo is polygynous. But it does not breed every year — only when there is likely to be an abundance of good food for chick-rearing, and this abundance is variable and unpredictable.

Observation of plants that kakapo have fed on combined with detailed analysis of the birds' droppings tells us that kakapo eat a vast range of leaves, fruits and seeds, from forest floor to treetop and from streambank to ridgetop. But the birds never intentionally depart from their totally vegetarian diet.

Leading its solitary life the kakapo stays within its home range most of the time. Home ranges may overlap but, because the birds wander around in the dark, we have never seen what happens when two birds meet. Like other birds the kakapo seems to announce its presence — by raucous screeches rather than song — but the purpose of these sounds is not yet understood.

Before man arrived the kakapo ranged throughout the mainland, from the north to the far south, from sea level to the upper limits of vegetation, in shrublands as well as in forests. Today the kakapo survives in very small numbers in only a few remote parts of the country — Fiordland, Stewart Island, Codfish Island and Little Barrier Island.

The kakapo is now so rare and its habitat so modified that we may, in fact, not be seeing the true natural life-style of the bird. Only when a kakapo population reaches full numbers again will this be known.

KIORE

To the Brink of Extinction

According to early Maori accounts, when the first humans, the forbears of the Maori, arrived in New Zealand a thousand or more years ago and began to settle, they found kakapo throughout the mainland. The birds were easy to catch and afforded good eating for the new settlers. The catching was done with dogs, snares, pit traps, on moonlit nights when a particular kakapo food source was abundant, or when the birds were at their whawharua or breeding ground. Being large and abundant, the kakapo was one of the birds the Maoris considered worth preserving. After being cooked it was placed in a gourd and covered with melted fat.

Kakapo skins also were of value to the Maori — as a kahu kakapo, a dress cape worn over the shoulders — and dried kakapo heads were worn as ear ornaments. In pre-European times North Island Maori, after kakapo had declined in their part of the country, occasionally made expeditions to the South Island to procure, among other things, kakapo skins.

The decline in the number of kakapo as a result of hunting was accelerated by disturbance of the bird's habitat, directly or indirectly.

The Maori's ancestors had brought with them the kiore, or Polynesian rat, described by some as the harmless little vegetarian rat. But the kiore is mostly vegetarian now only because its kind has depleted the available meat. The kiore may not be large enough or strong enough to eat many kakapo eggs or chicks. It is, however, certainly capable of reducing important food sources of the kakapo by eating fruits, leaves and seeds. This competition for food would have been most noticeable in autumn when kiore populations often reach very high numbers and kakapo are trying to feed their chicks.

Accidentally, or for good reason, the Maori also burned large tracts of forest, particularly in the North Island, thus further reducing kakapo habitat.

Early in the nineteenth century European settlers began adding to the destruction of habitat by burning and clear felling further tracts of forest for farming and timber. And with the Europeans came cats, two more kinds of rat, deer, pigs and all the farm animals which now also live in the wild. Once in the wild these were animals which either preyed upon birds or competed for, or damaged, their food sources and habitats. More introductions of damaging exotic species were to follow in later years.

The kiore (*Rattus exulans*) is the smallest of the three species of rat now present in New Zealand. It was one of the first predatory land mammals introduced by man, arriving with Polynesian settlers more than 1000 years ago. It had, and continues to have, a significant adverse effect on birdlife, by eating small eggs and chicks and depleting food sources.

Many of the introduced animals could, individually, have caused the total extermination of the kakapo over varying periods of time. In combination their effect has been catastrophic for kakapo as well as for more than 50 other birds and animals which are native to New Zealand.

By 1840 there were so few kakapo left in the North Island that sightings of them were worthy of comment. Rats, feral cats and forest destruction brought about by man seemed to be ensuring their eventual extinction.

The accelerated decline of the kakapo in the South Island must have started at the same time as in the north but, with steeper terrain there and less hunting and modification of the land by Maoris and Europeans, the decline of kakapo was slower in the more remote areas, and especially so where colder and wetter climatic conditions slowed the spread of introduced predators.

The early European explorers, particularly of Westland and Fiordland, must have been partially responsible for the decline of the kakapo, for during their journeys they depended on kakapo, and any other birds which their dogs could catch, for their meat supply. While few dogs would eat a weka, kea or kiwi, they never refused a kakapo. In Fiordland in about 1880, one explorer, and collector, Andreas Reischek, noted '. . . the birds used to be in dozens round the camp, screeching and yelling like a lot of demons, and at times it was impossible to sleep for the noise. The dog had to be tied up or matters would have been worse. It would have been killing and fetching all night long. . . .' But explorers soon noted, without too much regret for the birds, that their dogs could no longer find enough birds to keep expedition parties supplied with meat.

At this time the kakapo was also regarded as a valuable exhibition animal. There were many attempts to send live birds to zoos around the world. Despite the kakapo's value, however, the capture, caging and transportation methods used by collectors were horrendous by present standards. Half a dozen, or more, kakapo found by a muzzled dog or knocked out of a tree at night would be bundled together in a sack and carted back to camp. Often these birds would all be put into a few or very small cages. By morning some would be dead, owing to shock, or would have been killed by their own kind in the close confines of the cage. Food supplies for the caged birds seldom bore any resemblance to their natural diet — bread, potatoes and household scraps were commonplace. During transportation the birds were treated more like domestic poultry and, except on rare occasions, never reached their destination, having died en route, been so poorly that they were dumped ashore, or having escaped from the cages only to fall into the sea and drown.

Kakapo were also sometimes kept as pets, in a small cage or on a perch, being fed on household scraps. Few birds lived as long as one year.

Collecting specimens of bird species for museums, or merely to sell at a profit, was also common practice in the nineteenth century. Today we know of many hundreds of kakapo specimens in museums around the world and, if the recorded actions of a few collectors can be taken as representative, many hundreds more were killed and the specimens not prepared or the skins lost. The collectors correctly observed that kakapo numbers were declining but

Red Deer *Cervus elaphus scoticus*
The red deer is one of ten deer species introduced to New Zealand as game animals between 1851 and 1923. It is the species most commonly found in forests throughout the country. By browsing on and hence reducing or eliminating the most palatable plants, the deer have had, and continue to have, a profound adverse effect on forests and birdlife.

their greatest concern then was to preserve as many skins as possible before the remaining birds disappeared.

The final blow was struck in the early 1880s when ferrets, stoats and weasels were released in large numbers to combat the plague of rabbits which was devastating pastoral lands. The ferrets were bred and released by the hundreds. Stoats and weasels were given less assistance, but flourished naturally. In the 1890s rat numbers reached a high peak and doubtless provided an excellent food source for the newly liberated mustelids, particularly the stoat. By 1900 stoats, which proved to be the greatest threat to kakapo, had reached the most remote parts of mainland New Zealand and islands that were within swimming distance. Easily falling prey to the mustelids, many native species declined in number; only a handful remained unaffected. Kakapo numbers plummeted but there were few humans who noticed and even fewer who cared.

Feral Cat *Felis catus*

Apart from its wild habitat, the feral cat is no different from the common household cat. It is an efficient predator and, to satisfy its daily food requirements, needs many small food items, such as insects and mice, or a few larger items, such as birds and rats. Cats were probably first brought to New Zealand by early European sealers and whalers and, when abandoned in forest areas, quickly became wild. The effect of feral cats on birdlife has been disastrous—they have contributed to the extermination of a number of native species and continue to endanger more.

Stoat *Mustela erminea*

One of the more destructive ground predators now existing in New Zealand is the stoat. It was introduced in 1882 to control rabbits but it had little effect on them. It did, however, contribute significantly to the extermination of many bird species. The stoat eats insects, mice and rats as well. Being a skilful climber, it hunts just as efficiently in trees as it does on the ground and can also swim across wide areas of water, sometimes distances of more than a kilometre.

A Glimmer of Hope

One glimmer of hope for the endangered kakapo, by the 1890s thought to be surviving in reasonable numbers only in Fiordland, was the government appointment in 1894 of Richard Henry as official curator of Resolution Island. This remote island in Dusky Sound had been set aside in 1875 as 'a station to be used for the restraint and safe keeping of male offenders under sentence of penal servitude'. It was never used for that purpose and, following public pressure, was reserved in 1891 for the 'Protection of Native Flora and Fauna'. It is now part of Fiordland National Park.

Richard Henry was a bushman of Irish birth who had come to New Zealand from Australia some time in the 1870s. As a result of years spent in the Australian outback and in the New Zealand bush, he had become a keen naturalist. He also had experience in collecting birds. In the 1880s, as he became aware of the destructive effects that introduced predators were having on native birdlife, he turned his attention to matters of conservation. Henry's enthusiasm for wildlife and concern for its survival made him an ideal choice for curator of Resolution Island.

Henry foresaw the value of islands as predator-free refuges for vulnerable flightless birds and spent the following six years, with the help of one assistant (whom he paid from his own wage), studying, capturing and moving kakapo and kiwi from Fiordland forests to Resolution and other islands in Dusky Sound. In all he moved more than 700 birds. Considering the difficulties he had to endure with Fiordland's inclement weather conditions, sometimes working on his own, and finding and catching the birds — even if they were 'plentiful' they could still climb trees — this was a remarkable feat.

Henry's dream of saving the kakapo from extinction by transporting birds to islands in Dusky Sound was shattered, however, when he saw a 'weasel' on Resolution in 1900. Henry referred to all members of the mustelid family as 'weasels' but it is more likely that he had in fact seen a stoat.

Nevertheless, Henry continued his work to improve the situation of the kakapo and other birds until he resigned as curator of Resolution in 1908. He transferred birds to smaller islands in the Sound and sent some to aviaries. In 1903 four birds were taken from Resolution Island on the Government Steamer *Hinemoa* and liberated on Little Barrier Island, a reserve north-east of Auckland, which had been set aside for the 'Preservation of Native Fauna' in 1895. The birds were not seen again. What sex they were and what condition they were in when they were released is not known. Wild cats were present on Little Barrier at the time and remained a threat to all birds there until the last cat was removed in 1980 by Wildlife Service staff and helpers.

Largely as a result of the presence of stoats, the kakapo did not establish a colony on Resolution Island. But Henry's work in Fiordland was not a complete failure. With few exceptions his observations of the hard-to-observe nocturnal kakapo were amazingly accurate. Scientists of the day ignored or scorned many of his statements but today they support our observations and contribute significantly to our knowledge of the species.

In 1912 three kakapo were liberated on Kapiti Island, another wildlife reserve, a few kilometres off the North Island's south-west coast. These birds must have come from Resolution Island or Fiordland but it is not known how they were caught and transferred nor what condition they were in when they were released. Quite remarkably, at least one of these birds survived on the island until 1936. At the time of the birds' liberation the forests of Kapiti were struggling to recover from an era of felling and burning that was part of the many attempts by Europeans to create farmland.

Most of Kapiti Island had been made a reserve in 1897 with farm stock removed soon after. But goats, possums, wild sheep, cats and Norway rats were still present when the kakapo were liberated. The wild sheep were removed within a short time and the goats and cats were all gone by 1934. The possums have only recently been removed, in the 1980s, in a commendable effort organised by staff of the Department of Lands and Survey (staff now working within the Department of Conservation). The rats remain a threat to any further liberations on Kapiti.

After Richard Henry left Fiordland in 1908 nothing further was done to care for the remaining kakapo for another 50 years.

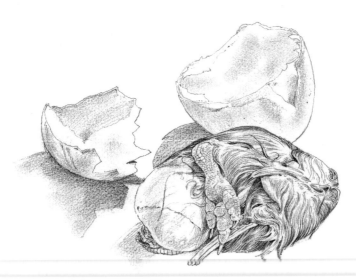

This Stewart Island kiwi chick had died in the egg. The well-developed state of the chick suggests that it would have hatched within a week or so. In most species, chicks have an egg tooth on the tip of their bill to help them chip their way out of the shell. The bill of a kiwi chick, however, is soft and flexible so the bird uses a toe to crack the shell.

Little Spotted Kiwi *Apteryx owenii*

Before the arrival of cats and mustelids, the little spotted kiwi — the smallest and, today, the rarest of New Zealand's three kiwi species — occurred throughout much of the South Island. The introduction of this species to Kapiti Island early this century has saved it from extinction. More recently, birds have been transferred from Kapiti to other islands.

Remnant Population — Fiordland

In the late 1950s interest in the kakapo was rekindled and Wildlife Service staff searched for birds in many valleys near Fiordland's Milford Sound. Earlier reports of kakapo being once numerous in this rugged region and knowledge of the distribution of introduced animals there suggested that this was the most likely area in which to still find a number of birds.

By 1959 kakapo were known to be remaining in the Tutoko Valley with possibly a few birds in nearby valleys. The only way considered practical to save the species from extinction was to take some birds into captivity. Using specially constructed cage traps and trained dogs, muzzled to safeguard the birds, five kakapo were caught in the Tutoko Valley. These birds were put into the care of Elwyn Welch, a keen amateur aviculturalist who had aviaries at Mount Bruce, near Masterton, in the lower North Island. Within a very short time three of the birds died — probably as a result of stress, mishandling during transfer, domestic avian diseases or the birds' refusal to eat most foods offered.

The first aviaries of Mount Bruce Native Bird Reserve (now the National Wildlife Centre of the Department of Conservation), constructed by the Wildlife Service on reserve land near the property of Elwyn Welch, were then ready for use, so the two remaining birds were transferred there. One died soon after, having lived in captivity for little more than a year; the other lived for a further two and a half years. The five birds taken from the Tutoko Valley were all males so there was no chance of them breeding anyway.

Further searches of valleys in Fiordland revealed fewer and fewer signs of kakapo.

In 1974, using as transport helicopters newly introduced for commercial deer-meat recovery, Wildlife Service staff were able to search cirques, hanging valleys and high alpine benches formerly out of reach to parties on foot. Two-man teams, each equipped with tent, primus cooker and other essentials, were airlifted to likely, but previously inaccessible, kakapo areas.

Almost without exception, campsites were at or above the bush line. Some were on such steep country that a helicopter could not touch a skid to the ground. Camping conditions were far from comfortable, with rain expected

Field workers' camp at the edge of Lake Liz in the Transit Valley, Fiordland, looking south-west, with the peak of 'Kakapo Kastle' on the left. The massive rock pinnacle of the 'Kastle' was given its name in the 1970s when two male kakapo were found to be using it as a site from which to make their booming, or mating, calls.

on every second day and at least one good fall of snow each trip, even in mid summer. Tales of tents torn in half by high winds, days spent in wet clothes, flooding on sloping ground, gear lost down steep inclines, falls out of helicopter slings, and harassment by keas and wekas were not uncommon.

The hardships of living and working in such inhospitable terrain were softened by the area's spectacular scenery and wonderful wildflowers in places yet to be reached by deer but, above all, by signs of more kakapo, which enabled us to add to our knowledge of this incredible bird.

Over the next four years, summer-time searches with trained dogs, attempts to observe the birds at night with night-vision scopes, special remote controlled traps, tape recordings of kakapo sounds and visits to kakapo areas in mid winter revealed a total of at least 18 kakapo — all males. The birds were still mainly in the Milford and nearby catchments — an area that was an 'ecological

Signs left by kakapo
1. Kakapo droppings are distinct in their shape and texture.
2. 'Chews' are spat out by kakapo after they have extracted the soft matter from fibrous leaves such as this *Olearia colensoi*.
3. The chewed growing part of the leaf bases of *Ghania procera*.

island' which, because of almost sheer mountain walls on all sides, had, at that time, resisted the spread of the alien animals already well established in most other mainland areas. Deer and possums were absent or in low numbers. Stoats were present but at high altitudes their numbers were significantly smaller than at lower levels. Even prior to the arrival of stoats and deer, kakapo numbers may have been higher closer to the snow line, where avalanches occasionally flatten areas of forest and hence create 'gardens' containing a large variety of regenerating, heavily fruiting vegetation.

High on a spur at the head of the Sinbad Valley, more than 1000 metres above sea level, were three male kakapo. Here, for the first time since Richard Henry had observed kakapo 75 years before, kakapo were seen attempting to breed. But there were no females.

Hope remained high but we also knew that, for their own safety, some birds had to be removed from Fiordland to a stoat-free island. To provide a transit camp for the birds that were to be transferred we built an aviary in the wet Fiordland forest, made comfortable dry places in it for kakapo to roost and stocked it with the best food-plants.

Above: Kakapo grubbing area
Right: Plant and other matter around the grubbing site
A. Carpet clubmoss — eaten for starch
B. Manuka root
C. Wire rush
D. Divot of turf removed by the bird's bill.

In the Esperance Valley was one bird which we optimistically named Jill. But was it really Jill, or John? Richard Henry had been quite emphatic that females were smaller, but recent measurements of all museum specimens in the world which were labelled as female had shown that they were not clearly different from the specimens labelled male. We know now that, because a pair of birds fetched a higher price, some of the specimen collectors simply labelled their birds male and female. In fact, the bulk and body weights of male and female kakapo are markedly different, but most of the standard measurements — such as foot, wing and tail length — are similar.

'Jill' was a little lighter and appeared smaller than other kakapo we knew, so into the safety of the aviary she went.

High on the wall of the Gulliver Valley was a tiny patch of forest, with close to 1000 metres of cliff below it and rock, snow and ice above. It seemed unlikely that any human had ever been there. The foot-slogging kakapo hunters of earlier days had eyed the precipitous area with frustration. Within a few minutes of stepping off the helicopter skid — this was a place where it could not touch the ground — we found kakapo sign. This was the home of a single male kakapo. He was so alone and so far from other kakapo that he too — now named Richard Henry — went into the aviary.

Early in 1976 in the Transit Valley, the next catchment south of Milford Sound, two teams working over a period of four weeks located four male kakapo, two of them high on a rock pinnacle 1000 metres above the valley floor with a view of the whole valley and Lake Liz. This pinnacle became known as 'Kakapo Kastle'. In our camp down by the lake the booming of the birds could be heard all night long, every night. Even when 25 millimetres of rain fell in one night (10 to 15 millimetres was more common) the birds continued to boom. But no females were found there.

With no more females known to exist in Fiordland, what more could we do for the surviving birds? Early in 1987 we knew of just five male kakapo remaining in Fiordland.

While man can find signs that kakapo are present in an area, to capture a bird is very difficult, particularly as few kakapo occur in any one area. Dogs, especially those trained to point or set, are invaluable in helping to find the birds. As the kakapo, with no flight muscles, has a weak rib cage, each dog is muzzled to ensure that it does not attempt to retrieve a bird. A bell worn by the dog assists the operator in following its activities for, although working within close proximity, the dog is often not visible in dense vegetation.

Overleaf: The rocky outcrop of 'Kakapo Kastle' towers above Lake Liz and stands 1000 metres above the floor of the Transit Valley. In breeding years kakapo continue to boom from this prominent place.

Rock Wren   *Xenicus gilviventris*

The rock wren is an alpine species found only in the South Island and, living above the bush line, it remains relatively safe from predators. The male bird is very confiding and curious, often coming within a few feet of its observer. The female seems less confiding, responding to disturbance with more frequent and agitated bobbing of her body.

Kea   *Nestor notabilis*

Although the kea is the alpine relative of the kakapo, it is able to fly and has an omnivorous diet and is thus much more able to adapt to man-modified New Zealand. It occurs naturally only in unforested areas above the bush line of the South Island — well away from most of the influences of man. Nevertheless, kea numbers are declining in many areas, largely as a result of habitat modification.

South Island Robin *Petroica australis australis*
The South Island robin is cheeky enough to sit on a tramper's
boot and cunning enough to have survived, albeit in reduced
numbers, the depredations of rats, cats and mustelids. Feeding
only on insects, usually taken on the ground, the robin appears
to be little affected by the deer- and possum-induced changes
to the forest. Populations of this subspecies are scattered
throughout much of the South Island.

Opposite: A selection of alpine plants now rarely seen in areas
browsed by deer. *Lower left:* Maori onion (*Bulbinella gibbsii*);
centre left: Alpine gentian (*Gentiana patula*); *centre:* Mountain
daisy (*Celmisia verbascifolia*).

Kiwis share the forest and the night with kakapo and the young birds are just as defenceless as kakapo chicks. Kiwi chicks, like the three-week-old brown kiwi (*Apteryx australis*) illustrated below, receive little or no protection from their parents so are particularly vulnerable to predation by animals such as the stoat, which can easily enter a nest, as visualised opposite.

Yellow crowned parakeet chick

Adult and chick

This chick was being fed just prior to its first flight from the nesthole.

Chicks have a pinky fawn bill and grey cere whereas the adults have a bluish bill and red cere.

Kakariki *Cyanoramphus spp.*

The kakariki, or parakeet, is New Zealand's smallest parrot. Unlike the entirely vegetarian kakapo, the kakariki, in common with the kaka and the kea, is an omnivore. Being small and able to feed economically on seeds and insects, it can find enough food to rear perhaps two broods of two to four chicks each summer. In the 1800s, when it developed a taste for orchard fruits, the red-crowned parakeet (*C. novaezelandiae*) was numerous enough to be considered a nuisance. Today, largely as a result of predation by rats and stoats, it is rarely seen in mainland forests. The yellow-crowned parakeet (*C. auriceps*) is now more common than the red-crown but it is declining in number, also because of predation.

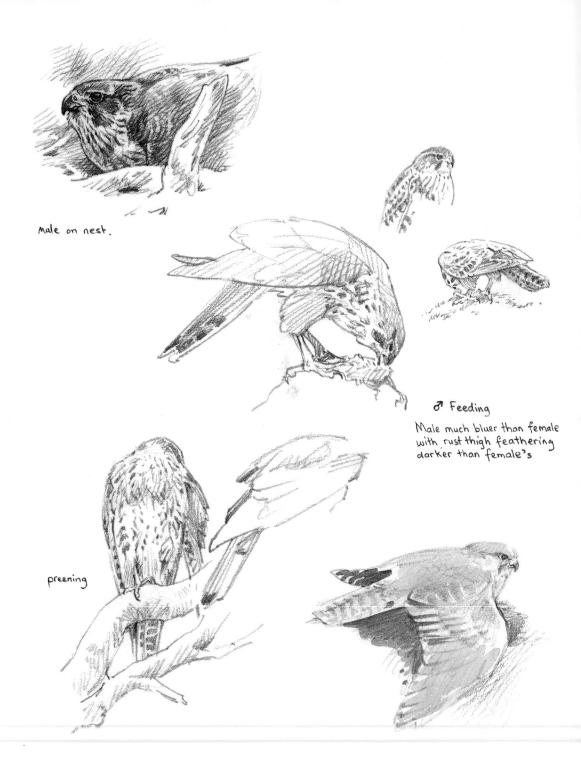

Male on nest.

♂ Feeding

Male much bluer than female
with rust thigh feathering
darker than female's

preening

New Zealand Falcon   *Falco novaeseelandiae*
Although rarely seen, the New Zealand falcon is widespread and, compared with
falcons in other parts of the world, quite common in larger forest areas where it feeds
mainly on small birds, rodents and large insects.

New Zealand Falcon –
Adult female

Silvereye *Zosterops lateralis*

Tauhou (stranger) was the name given by the Maori to this comparatively recent arrival in New Zealand. The silvereye appeared in pre-European times, coming presumably from Australia. It is now found throughout mainland New Zealand and on offshore islands, but it is more at home in shrubland and gardens than in mature forest. When silvereyes are common in forest areas it is a sure indicator that the forest has been modified — by browsing animals or by burning.

48

Blue Duck   *Hymenolaimus malacorhynchos*

The blue duck was once a common bird of the clear and unpolluted streams of forested areas throughout most of New Zealand. Destruction of most of the forests by both man and browsing animals has resulted in siltation of streams and depletion of the blue duck's food supply of aquatic insects. The bird is now restricted to forested mountain areas.

Male Blue Duck —

A brooding fantail looks agitated as a feeding family of riflemen forages at the base of her nesting tree.

Fantail *Rhipidura fuliginosa*

By virtue of its aerial feeding habits and its choice of the slenderest branches as nest sites, the fantail has avoided predators and remains a relatively common bird of the forest and shrublands throughout much of New Zealand. It has also adapted well to larger suburban gardens. So 'tame' has the fantail become that it will even enter buildings, hovering about in its characteristic erratic flight with tail constantly fanned. Belonging to the family of flycatchers, the fantail eats only insects.

Yellowhead sketches

When feeding amongst moss-
covered tree trunks the birds
will often spread their feet
wide, displacing the moss to
reveal the insects underneath

The stiff tail feather shafts
are bare at the tip and
often used to support the birds
when foraging vertically

ankles held close
together and far
back on body

At the end of the female's song,
the strong slow rattle makes the
tail feathers spread apart in a
very distinctive way.

Yellowhead *Mohoua ochrocephala*
The yellowhead—nicknamed 'bush canary' for its colour and chattering song—was once a common sight in South Island forests. The bird's hole-nesting habits restrict it to mature forests and make it vulnerable to predation by rats and stoats. Destruction of the forest understorey has depleted its source of insect food in many areas.

Opposite
Long-tailed Cuckoo *Eudynamys taitensis*
Each spring, for its breeding season, the long-tailed cuckoo migrates to New Zealand from islands in the western Pacific. The cuckoo, however, neither builds a nest nor rears its young; the female lays single eggs in the nests of other small birds. In the North Island the cuckoo's preferred host for the rearing of its chicks is the whitehead (*Mohoua albicilla*) and in the South Island it chooses the yellowhead. Usually the timing of the cuckoo's egg laying is such that the newly hatched cuckoo chick is able to push the host's unhatched eggs or small young out of the nest. In the nest illustrated above—belonging to yellowheads—the timing was not right and the host parents reared both the cuckoo chick and one of their own chicks.

53

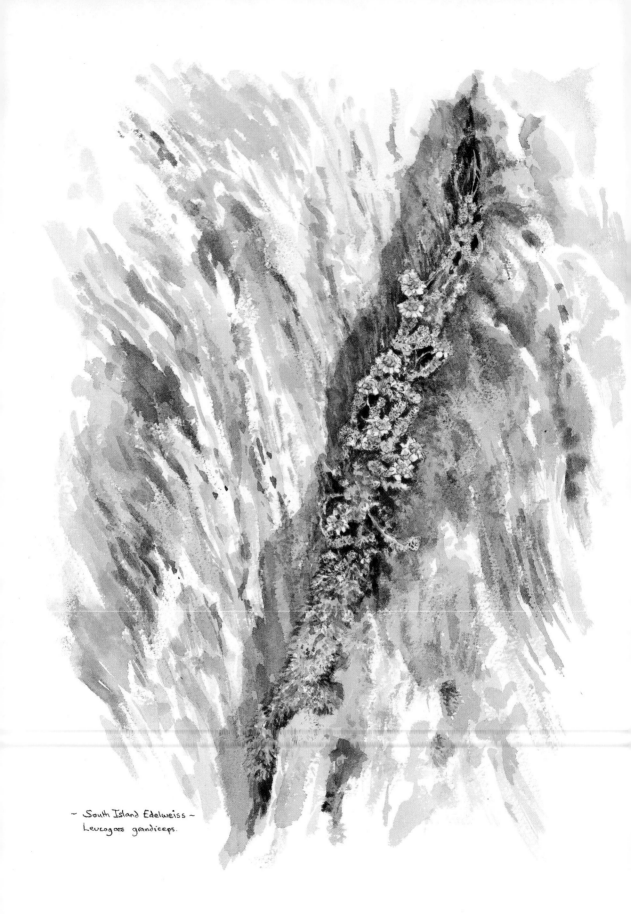

~ South Island Edelweiss ~
Leucogenes grandiceps.

Fiordland Skink (Leiolopisma acrinasum)

A Stop-gap — Maud Island

It is known that kakapo cannot co-exist with predatory animals, and that each bird likes to have a large home range. There are no suitable kakapo habitats on the mainland and few of New Zealand's 700 offshore and outlying islands have escaped colonisation by some sort of pest. Even fewer islands have habitats remotely similar to the natural forest habitat of the kakapo.

One island that did seem suitable, at least as a temporary home for kakapo, was Maud Island, a reserve right inside the Marlborough Sounds, at the north-eastern extremity of the South Island. Despite years of farming, wartime occupation as a gun site, barges loaded with timber and produce pulling up alongside the wharf and many boats visiting, there were no introduced predators — not even mice.

Although sheep graze much of the island and there are groves of introduced pine trees scattered around, a small area of native bush remains on the steep slopes behind the farmhouse. With food available from this forest remnant, supplementary feed of seeds and fruit, water-supply troughs (specially designed for kakapo) and food trees planted for future use, Maud was an adequate refuge for kakapo — just like an aviary, but without wire-netting, for these flightless birds could not escape. And the island was small enough for them to be managed.

During 1974 and 1975 'Richard Henry', 'Jill' and one other bird were shifted from the Fiordland aviary to Maud Island. Later, two more birds from Fiordland and four, including two females, from the newly discovered Stewart Island population were moved but, sadly, one bird did not survive the trip. By now it was known that 'Jill' was really 'John' so Maud Island's kakapo population comprised six males and two females.

In 1980 Maud Island became home also for the South Island saddleback, a native bird long since gone from all of the South Island but now reintroduced from islands near Stewart Island. The species' rapid disappearance from Maud, however, indicated that something was wrong — stoats had swum from the one-kilometre-distant mainland. By that time, 1982, Little Barrier Island had been cleared of cats so 'Richard Henry', the two female kakapo and the only other male remaining on Maud shifted house yet again.

The small remnant of forest on Maud Island was probably left intact to protect the farmhouse below it from land slips. The discovery on the island of the rare native Hamilton's frog (*Leiopelma hamiltoni*) and the successful introduction of a rare giant weta demonstrates the value of even small areas of forest for the conservation of endangered species. The arrival of stoats on Maud in 1982, however, curtailed use of the island as a sanctuary for birds.

Remnant Population —
Stewart Island

Kakapo must have always been on Stewart Island, despite its harsh climate, but they were rarely mentioned by early explorers and naturalists. It is also surprising that the tin miners and others who lived and worked over much of the southern half of Stewart Island from the 1880s to the 1940s, did not record the presence of kakapo which must have been quite numerous at that time. Indeed, reports of birds were so rare that nobody believed a young deer hunter who, in 1949, caught a kakapo and, just to prove that he had done so, plucked some feathers from it and sent them to the Wildlife Service.

In 1977 the National Provident Fund granted funds to the Wildlife Service to search for kakapo in new areas. As some searching had already been done in most mainland areas, the south of Stewart Island was chosen as being the most remote and least known area. Surprisingly, kakapo were readily found. Further careful searches revealed a population of more than 100, possibly 200, birds in the south-east part of the island. The presence of such a relatively large population was probably due to the fact that stoats, the worst enemy of kakapo, were never introduced to Stewart Island.

Some of the forest in the areas where kakapo were found was burnt years ago so that now there are areas of regenerating shrublands interspersed with pockets of podocarp forest which were missed by the fires. This type of environment might not be considered as the natural home of the kakapo, but the regenerating forest, along with the natural forest diversity due to soil types and landform, may offer a greater variety of food in a smaller area than did the original forest.

Later surveys in the same areas, however, showed that the kakapo were rapidly disappearing — largely as a result of predation by cats. The cats had been on the island for a long time and must have been taking their toll of kakapo, but in previous years they had enjoyed a more plentiful supply of other birds — wekas and, around the coast, sooty shearwaters. Having reduced the numbers of wekas and shearwaters to a low level, the cats had to find other food and, apart from a seasonal abundance of rats, kakapo were virtually all that there was.

Kakapo were, nonetheless, still numerous enough on the island for us to have some idea of the sights and sounds that greeted early explorers of the

---

View from Arena Ridge, south-east Stewart Island, looking north over kakapo habitat to the exfoliating granite domes of Trig I.

West Coast and Fiordland. Screeches, which can only be likened to a play actor being slowly murdered, rent the night air and, when the males decided it was a good year for breeding and began to gather in groups and boom, ten or more birds could be heard at one time. The Maori hunting lore 'Never take the bird which is being danced around — take only the ones that are dancing' began to gain credence.

And there were females — clearly smaller in size than the males, just half to three-quarters of the male's weight, with slimmer faces and scratchier temperaments. Among the first found were 'Nora', in a nest under tussock bushes with three chicks, and 'Alice', with a single chick — now named 'Snark' — in an underground nest.

Snark and two of Nora's chicks survived to fledge but other kakapo did not fare so well. In one year the corpses of ten cat-killed kakapo were found. Finding that number of birds among the thick scrub suggested that many, many more had been killed. Between their discovery in 1977 and 1982, more than 50 per cent of the kakapo which had been marked to assist scientists in studying the population were killed by cats.

In 1982, in a desperate bid to avert a critical situation, 18 Stewart Island kakapo were shifted to the now safe Little Barrier Island. Cat hunters were hired and, with every method possible, they set out to reduce the number of cats in the kakapo area of southern Stewart Island, and the hunting continues. The hunters' working conditions are reminiscent of those of the earliest gold miners: living in tiny tin huts that never see the sun, walking for hour after hour on muddy tracks, in rain, hail or shine. As the hunters are few in number, however, their work is limited to a relatively small part of the island. To remove, or even control, the cats over a larger area would be a much too costly task.

Cat hunting on Stewart Island is very much a stop-gap measure, but the hunters are continuing to keep cat numbers so low that, so far as we can tell, no kakapo have been killed in recent years. The situation remains precarious though, for if the basic food source for the cats — rats — should suddenly decline, there will be some very hungry cats quite capable of walking the few kilometres into the kakapo area overnight.

In mid-1987 we were aware of just 29 birds on Stewart Island — four females and 25 males — and work has begun to move these to the safety of nearby Codfish Island.

Following two pages: The home ranges of some of the kakapo of southern Stewart Island in January 1987. The reason that the birds have survived in this remote area may well be that the original forest burnt over by tin miners became a good habitat of regenerating shrubland for kakapo, but a poor one for cats.

Found at 1.00p.m - 19th Jan 87.

right foot

Tara, the short-haired German pointer kakapo dog,
found this unbanded male bird in a sheltered
hollow under a dracophyllum stump.
  Unbanded birds are a rare find these days
as most kakapo are known from previous
expeditions, so it was a real thrill to find him.
He was named after our expedition leader, Ralph.

TIN RANGE

Sass

Lionel

Alice

Ge

'Nora', a female Kakapo found
on Bench Hill near Scolley's Flat.
21 Jan 87.

Foot detail - right leg.
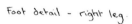

Fer

From field observations some birds have
brownish grey feet while others have waxy
cobalt blue feet. I wondered if the bluer
feet indicate a younger bird.

Male

Strong grooves on the underside and
inside of both mandibles probably help
in the mastication and break-up of food.

Kakapo are strong climbers and are
quite at home foraging for food or
roosting in trees.

65

Some plant species upon which Kakapo feed

a. Mingimingi (Cyathodes juniperina)   b. Manuka (Leptospermum scoparium)
c. Leatherwood (Olearia colensoi)   d. Rimu (Dacrydium cupressinum)

Found on the Tin Range, Stewart Island
27 · 1 · 87

Harlequin Gecko *Hoplodactylus rakiurae*
The harlequin gecko occurs only on Stewart Island and was not discovered there until 1979. Its colour pattern is unique among New Zealand lizards. Although nocturnal and ground dwelling, it will sometimes bask in the sun.

Water or Brown Rat *Rattus norvegicus*
The water rat is one of three local species of rat, all introduced into the country by man during the early years of exploration and settlement. It is thought to have arrived some time in the eighteenth century aboard European ships. The two other species are the black rat (*R. rattus*), which came also with early Europeans, and the kiore (*R. exulans*), which arrived with Polynesian settlers many years before. All three species became established throughout the mainland and on many offshore islands, causing the destruction of many native birds. They continue to destroy wildlife and, aided by careless human activities, can easily become established on islands where no rats are present.

   The rat illustrated above — a water rat — has been caught in a Fenn trap.

Opposite
Short-tailed Bat *Mystacina tuberculata*
Two species of bat — the short-tailed and the long-tailed — were the only land mammals in New Zealand before the arrival of man. Because of the adaptations of not having a flying membrane attached to its tail and of being able to completely fold away its wing membranes, the short-tailed species is unique among bats in being able to crawl around on the ground — the ecological niche usually occupied by rats. When European rats reached New Zealand they exterminated or greatly reduced the numbers of both bat species in most areas. The short-tailed bat is now the rarer of the two.

68

Harrier *Circus approximans*

The harrier is usually regarded as a scavenger, but, given the opportunity, is a predator of birds and small animals which are not fast enough to take evasive action. Before man reached New Zealand, the harrier was one of only two diurnal predators likely to affect the kakapo; the falcon was the other. Being a bird more of open country than forest, however, the harrier was not so numerous as it is now throughout the country.

Opposite

Morepork *Ninox novaeseelandiae*

The morepork, found throughout New Zealand, is the country's only surviving native owl. Although feeding largely on insects, it has adapted well to feed on the rats and mice introduced by man. When it has young to provide for, it may prey upon the chicks of other birds. Chicks in the 'hole' nests of kakapo are, however, quite safe.

The weka hunted amongst seaweed at the water's edge, sometimes catching fish which had been frightened from their hiding places

territorial threat posture

Weka   *Gallirallus australis*

The flightless weka may be classed as a predator, as it takes the eggs and chicks of other ground-dwelling birds. Kakapo, however, have co-existed with the weka for a very long time. Wherever wekas occur they can be heard calling at night but they are probably not very capable nocturnal hunters so kakapo chicks, guarded by the female during the day but left alone at night, are usually safe. In earlier times, when there were no large wild animals for man to hunt in the forest, the weka was an easy source of food for humans.

Stewart Island Brown Kiwi   *Apteryx australis lawryi*

The Stewart Island brown kiwi is the largest of the three brown kiwi subspecies. It appears to be less of a nocturnal bird than its northern relatives and in its forest or scrubland habitat may sometimes be seen foraging during daylight hours.

73

The Kakapo Breeding System

Most of the birds we know in our gardens, farms and forests live together as pairs, or pair for all or part of the breeding season and then join a flock for the winter, or a male has a harem. The kakapo does none of these things. And after mating it is the female alone who prepares a nest and raises the chicks, with no assistance from the male.

Since the male is not required by the female for more than the fertilisation of her eggs, he has the choice of accompanying an individual female until he is able to mate with her or of advertising his presence by calls and displays in the hope that he may mate with more than one female. The kakapo has chosen the latter course.

Perhaps being aware that there is not much point in separately advertising from a lonely hilltop if a group of males is gathered together on another hilltop, male kakapo gather together loudly advertising their presence and apparently vocally competing with one another for the favours of the females. In ornithological terms this gathering together of male birds in courtship competition is called a lek. For kakapo this may mean being no closer to one another than 50 metres — but still in a position to compete vocally.

To create the characteristic deep booming mating call made during the nocturnal competition, the male kakapo inflates air sacs which swell his breast and throat until he is the shape of a football. These air sacs then act as a resonating drum for a series of slightly drawn out grunts produced as the bird expels each breath. Although a seemingly soft call, the booming can readily be heard by humans within a kilometre or two of the booming site and has been heard from as far away as seven kilometres. The booming can continue all night, every night, for as long as three months. In one night a male may emit as many as 17,000 booms.

The 'stage' for the male's courtship performance is a bowl-like depression in the earth, excavated by the bird to fit the shape of his inflated half-metre-long body and meticulously cleared of twigs and vegetation each booming season. The bowl is often backed by a reflector of stone, tree-trunk or shrubbery to help project the booming out over the countryside. Early explorers called these depressions dusting bowls, but, given the constant high rainfall of Fiordland, it is doubtful that dust would ever form and we now know that the bowls are purely for courtship purposes.

From his booming bowl the male kakapo begins the courtship ritual by inflating his air sacs and repeatedly emitting a deep resonant booming note to announce to females that he is ready to mate.

Immediately around the bowl the ground is also meticulously cleared of vegetation and twigs. Joining this courtship station to others made by the same male, or just leading to the bowl, will usually be a number of tracks — again all meticulously cleared each booming season. This track and bowl system, usually sited in a prominent hilltop position, is the male's 'court' which the female must enter to mate with him.

Track and bowl systems are also visited by males in non-booming seasons and some clearance of twigs and vegetation is carried out. This clearing of the tracks and bowls is done by the bird tossing twigs and leaves aside each time he passes or by chewing small pieces into smaller fragments and dropping them back to the ground. Later, wind and rain blow or wash away these fragments so that old tracks become distinct depressions in the ground.

A breeding season does not occur each year, however, or even every second year. Richard Henry observed that the kakapo of Fiordland boomed, and hence bred, only in years when the tussock seeded well. He noted, wryly, that ornithologists would scorn this observation, and scorn it they did, but recent field work and studies, 85 years later and with the aid of modern technology, have shown just how right Henry was. It appears that the male kakapo booms when he can predict that two or three months after the booming begins there will be a good supply of food for the rearing of chicks. In reality it is more likely that the same series of weather patterns that results in a good fruiting year also causes the kakapo to feel fit and well and ready to breed.

The kakapo's breeding season, then, may occur at two-, three- or even four-year intervals. In New Zealand avifauna, and among parrots of the world, the kakapo's 'forecasting' ability is rare, although around the world, particularly in arid regions, many species breed in response to environmental cues such as rainfall or bumper food crops. The time of year when kakapo booming occurs appears to vary from place to place in keeping with the time of year when prime chick food will be available. On Stewart Island, booming sometimes starts in December and may continue into May, but a season from January to March is more usual and chick rearing coincides with the ripening of rimu fruit. On Little Barrier the males boomed for the first time in April and May of 1986, but no nesting occurred. We have yet to establish what food may be available there for chick rearing.

In order to grow, young animals need protein. Most birds obtain this for their young by feeding them insects. Parrots such as New Zealand's kakariki, kaka and kea eat insects as well as a basic diet of seeds and fruits. The kakapo, however, being strictly vegetarian, needs either large seeds or an abundance of small seeds. Plants do not produce this abundance every year.

Following two pages: The track and bowl system of one male kakapo in Fiordland, on the top of 'Kakapo Kastle' with a view to Lake Liz. In years gone by this area may have been used by a number of males. Today the single male uses at least eight different bowls (*far right of illustration, numbered in sequence from the left*). The arrow near the shore of the lake shows the location of the field workers' camp.

Track and bowl on Stewart Island — The crossed sticks in the bowl's centre were placed there by one of the survey team. If the male Kakapo was using the bowl the sticks would be displaced when it next visited. This bowl was used by 'Tramp' and measured 63 cm in diameter and 8 cm in depth.

The series of weather patterns, or other events of which we are not aware, which causes good seeding years for kakapo food-plants, also stimulates the male kakapo to come into breeding condition. The body weight of a male kakapo may increase by up to 60 per cent before booming commences. The females similarly respond to the environmental cues, come into breeding condition and visit the males at their leks. Endeavouring to be more appealing than his neighbour and so attract a female to his court, each male booms, screeches and displays. When a female appears, the male walks around rocking from side to side, spreading his wings and showing his mottled green back. This is the dance of the kakapo.

A female may walk many kilometres to visit a male, may mate once only and then return to her home range and lay a clutch of two, three or four small white eggs in a nest which, like that of other parrots, is situated in a 'hole'. For a parrot the size of a kakapo, however, holes may not be easy to find, so spaces under dense overhanging vegetation sometimes suffice. No building material is carried into the nest; the nest is created by the female simply grubbing up the floor of the chosen cavity and chewing up all the larger pieces of material that are already there to form a dry floor of sawdust-like consistency many centimetres deep.

Overall, were it not for the interference of predators and competitors introduced by man, the kakapo's breeding system would be ideal for such a large and long-lived bird. The last breeding season we observed on Stewart Island, in 1985, indicated how fragile the system is in present times. The male kakapo, and Wildlife Service scientists, predicted that it would be a good seeding year for the rimu trees — the prime food source for chicks there. The males boomed well and the females laid their eggs. But, when the chicks were a few weeks old, the development of seeds for food did not proceed as expected. The kakapo chicks died.

In the same season Alice showed us that our presumptions about the booming of the males attracting females may also be wrong. When she wanted to mate she walked from her home range *away* from the booming males to the place where she had mated three years previously, the year she had produced her chick Snark, only to find that there was no male there. Buster, her previous mate, had been eaten by a cat. Alice walked back to the nest she had prepared, laid four infertile eggs and incubated them just as if all were well.

The track and bowl system of a male kakapo — 'Lionel' — on Arena Ridge, Stewart Island.

Following six pages: Kakapo courtship.

'Lionel's' Track and Bowl System, Arena Ridge 3
This system is a half hour's uphill walk
s. west of Scolley's Flat.
Approx. 210 metres above sea level.

Key:—

Granite Knobs
Manuka, Rata, Dracophyllum
Gahnia tussock
Kakapo bowl
Kakapo track

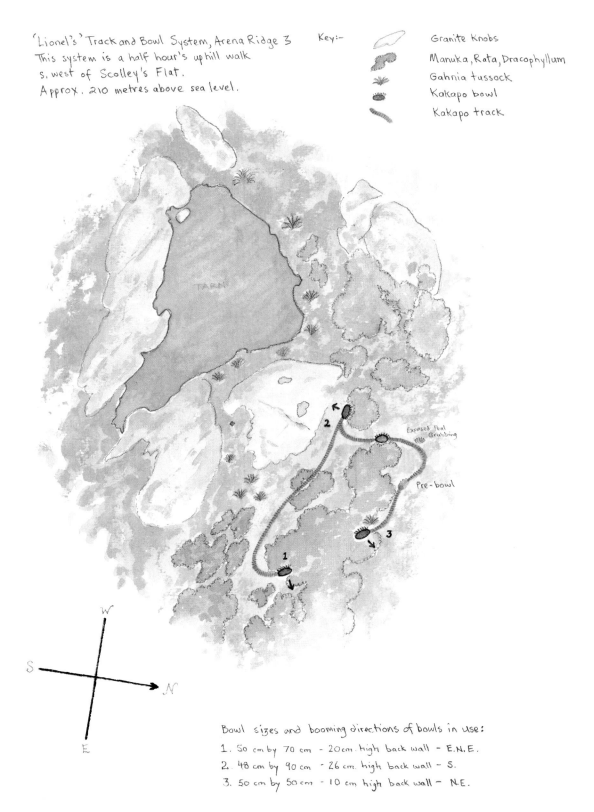

Bowl sizes and booming directions of bowls in use:
1. 50 cm by 70 cm - 20 cm. high back wall - E.N.E.
2. 48 cm by 90 cm - 26 cm. high back wall - S.
3. 50 cm by 50 cm - 10 cm high back wall - N.E.

When the male's booming has brought the
female within sight of the bowl,
he begins to dance.

At first, he rocks mechanically from one foot to the other, making low clicking
noises with his bill as he advances towards her.

As he gets closer to the female he begins to spread his wings which
are raised and lowered in a slow 'butterfly' display as he walks.

He begins to turn as he dances.

The full green beauty of his plumage
is paraded before the female in
the ritual wooing.

With wings wide-spread he backs towards her

Wingtips touching the ground and head
bent low in front of him, he stops.
The next move is hers.

Overleaf: The male displays as the female approaches.

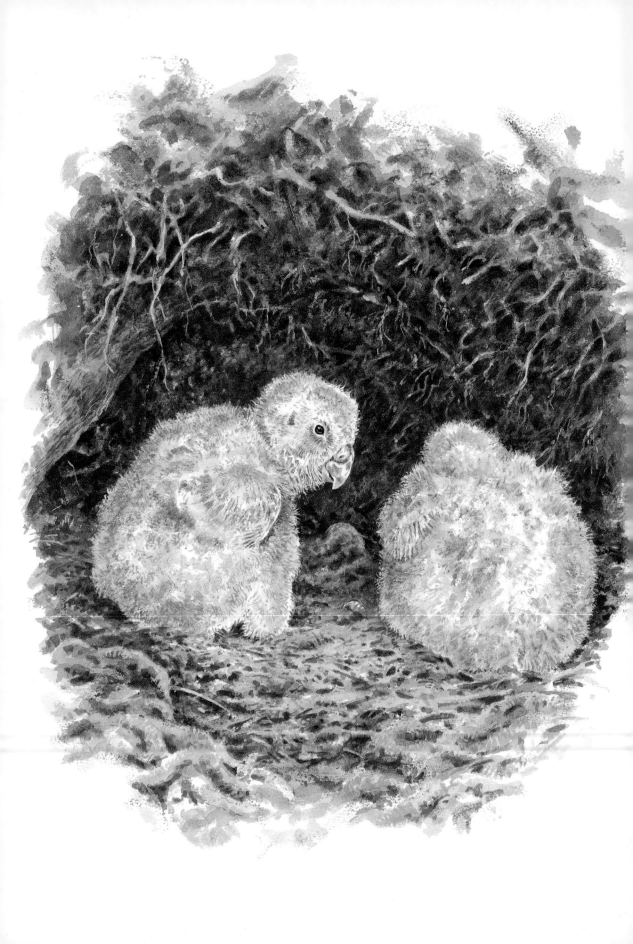

In the Nest and After

The female kakapo alone incubates her eggs and rears her chicks, going off for long periods each night to feed. When the chicks hatch, after about 30 days of incubation, the mother's feeding needs to be greater so that she can pass food on to her young. The chicks at this stage have a dense covering of white down and are helpless, but the female still leaves them for two- to three-hour spells on two or more occasions each night while she goes to feed.

Initially the young chicks are fed on the soft, rich, growing parts of plants such as the bases of *Dracophyllum* shoots. As the chicks grow and require more food, the female may walk many kilometres to gather protein-rich food such as the seeds of rimu or kahikatea. Usually she does this twice each night so that the chicks may be fed during the night. While the chicks are very young the mother has the ability to keep some food in her crop for further feeds for the chicks during the day, but after two weeks or so she will roost elsewhere by day and visit the nest to feed the chicks only at night.

The chicks' droppings stay at the edges of the nest cavity but, being vegetable matter, do not have an odour notably different from the surrounding forest, although to a dog, kakapo seem to have a very strong scent. Of greater attraction to predators is the frequent, and often continuous, grunting and squeaking made by the chicks. In addition to this, the frequent trips to and from the nest by the female must create a well-scented trail which can easily be located by a hungry cat.

After three months in the nest the chicks begin to move away from the nest site but for a further few weeks depend on the female for food. Then they wander off. On Stewart Island, Alice's chick Snark, whom we presumed to be typical, when one year old was found four kilometres from his nest site. Later, after establishing a regular home range, he still occasionally wandered as far away as nine kilometres. When the older males boomed he visited them, listened and watched. Snark is now six years old. Kakapo are undoubtedly very long-lived birds but we do not know how old Snark will be before he has a bowl of his own and begins to boom.

Kakapo chicks start life as down-covered helpless bodies. During the chick's three-month nestling period, feathers gradually grow to cover the down.

Southern Rata (Metrosideros umbellata)

Sun Orchid (Thelymitra venosa)

Yellow Silver Pine (Dacrydium intermedium)

A regular food eaten by Kakapo in winter months is the bulb of the Sun Orchid.
In summer and autumn it will readily climb trees to obtain nectar from Rata
flowers and the fruit of Yellow Silver Pine.

Opposite: 'Alice' feeding her chick 'Snark' (on Stewart Island). When he first emerged
from the nest, Snark, like other young kakapo, had a short tail and noticeably puffed
face feathers. At this stage his mother was walking to rimu trees two kilometres from
the nest to gather berries with which to feed him.

90

Alice feeding Snark

A Habitat Repaired — Little Barrier Island

Little Barrier Island today is as New Zealand was 300 years ago — forest clad and free of predators except for the kiore, the Polynesian rat brought to New Zealand by the Maori. In recent times the island has not always been so.

As well as indirectly disturbing the environment by introducing the kiore, the early Maori settlers on Hauturu — as Little Barrier was known to them — accidentally, or to create garden areas, burned parts of the island's native forest. The kiore may have exterminated small seabirds and ground-dwelling birds such as snipe, crakes and banded rails; they have certainly affected the numbers and variety of lizards and reduced the abundance of some plants. Later, with European visitors to the island, came cats. These, or perhaps only one pregnant female, got to Little Barrier in about 1870, became wild and soon populated the whole island. By 1890 the saddlebacks had been exterminated, other bird species reduced in number and hundreds of nesting seabirds were being eaten.

With many native species declining dramatically on the mainland throughout the latter part of the nineteenth century, early conservationists foresaw the value of Little Barrier as a bird sanctuary. The island was a large and isolated area of relatively intact native forest with little farming potential. After various manoeuvres by the principal parties — the Auckland Institute, Maori owners and government — which included notices of intent in the *New Zealand Gazette*, the selling of kauri-felling rights by the Maori owners, a court injunction, more *Gazette* notices and an Act of Parliament, the island was purchased by the Crown in 1894 and declared a reserve.

After that little changed. In 1897 a resident caretaker was installed. He trapped some cats and kiore, escorted permitted visitors and kept unwanted visitors away. There were various attempts to introduce or reintroduce native birds to the island but, because of the cats, only the introduction of kiwis was successful — it seems that kiwi meat is fairly well down on the cat's menu.

Ever since the establishment of Little Barrier as a reserve, conservationists have seen the tremendous value of islands as places where wildlife can survive while man continues to destroy mainland habitats. Little Barrier was the only

Mount Herekohu (the Thumb) and boulder beach, Little Barrier Island, seen from Te Titoki Point, the south-west corner of the island. Little Barrier's boulder beaches make any landing there by boat extremely difficult and thus help keep the island sanctuary secure.

place where the rare stitchbird survived, a last stronghold for Cook's and black petrels and home for a greater abundance than elsewhere of many other native species. But the cats were obviously continuing to reduce bird numbers and were preventing the use of Little Barrier as a haven for more species.

Between 1977 and 1980 scores of people, paid and unpaid, worked diligently to eradicate the total cat population, and succeeded. All the birds benefited and some species increased dramatically in number. With the cats removed, Little Barrier Island became not only safe for the return of species destroyed by the cats but could also be a home for species which continue to decline on the mainland. Being 3000 hectares in extent and rising to 720 metres above sea level, the island is large enough and has sufficient variety of vegetation to support all the species of birds which existed in similar forest areas on the mainland.

The kakapo was one of these species so, with Little Barrier being the only available large forested environment free of predators except for the kiore, 22 birds were transferred there in 1982 — 20 from Stewart Island and two from Fiordland, nine females and 13 males. They have survived well on Little Barrier, although, as regular checks showed, it took the birds all of a year to find their way about and learn to eat new foods. With the males in 1986 weighing less than 2 kilograms, they are a little lighter than the Stewart Island males, which weigh just over 2 kilograms, some reaching 2.5 to 3.0 kilograms in the summer of a booming year. Similarly the Little Barrier females weigh a little below the Stewart Island average of 1.5 kilograms. If one scientific hypothesis (Bergman's Rule) — that a species is heavier in a colder climate — can be applied here, then this weight difference can be expected to remain.

The summer of 1985/86 promised to be a good fruiting year for rimu and kahikatea — the plants traditionally fed on by chick-feeding females on Stewart Island — so for the first time on Little Barrier the males made bowls and boomed long and loud — just as they would have done on Stewart Island. Some females seemed to visit the males at their bowls but no nests were found. It was, indeed, a good year for fruiting of kahikatea and rimu but, for some unexplained reason, there are very few of these trees on Little Barrier. If kakapo are to breed on the island they will have to learn about new foods for chick feeding and how to predict when these foods will be sufficiently abundant for chick rearing.

Of the 22 birds which were transferred to Little Barrier in 1982, at least 16 are known to have survived to the winter of 1986.

Toropapa *Alseuosmia macrophylla*
Toropapa is a shrub difficult to find today on mainland New Zealand as deer and goats have eaten most of it. The species is still present on Little Barrier Island where nectar from the delightfully scented flowers is a favoured food of the stitchbird.

Giant Weta *Deinacrida heteracantha*
Measuring up to 100 millimetres in length, this giant weta, found only on Little Barrier Island, is one of the world's largest insects. It is also one of the heaviest, comparing in weight with a blackbird. This species is but a reminder of similar insects which were once present on the mainland. The weta is a largely nocturnal insect but the giant species of Little Barrier, unlike its smaller cousins, makes no attempt to dig a daytime roosting burrow in dead wood; it simply finds a convenient, and often not well-hidden, crevice. In unmodified habitats few, if any, animals or birds eat adult giant wetas but moreporks and kiore take the young.

Stitchbird   *Notiomystis cincta*

The male stitchbird is one of New Zealand's brighter coloured native birds. The 'stitch' part of the name refers not to 'sewing' (some species 'stitch' or 'weave' nests) but the bird's onomatopoeic alarm call. Stitchbirds were once found throughout the North Island and on Great and Little Barrier islands. They became extinct on the mainland by 1880 and today the only viable population is on Little Barrier. Attempts to establish new populations on other islands have met with little success owing to the wide altitudinal range needed to afford food for the birds during varying weather cycles.

96

Female Stitchbird

These three stitchbird chicks begged loudly
for food whilst still in their resthole, but
on fledging sat silently amongst the leaf
cover even when being fed. This made them
difficult to find, perhaps a useful guard
against predators.

Kokako love to eat
Bag moth pupae and squeeze
them like emptying a tube of
toothpaste.

general colour—

warm grey
wings brown tint.
tail darker towards tip
downward curve to tail feathers
legs & feet dk grey.
tarsees thinner than expected
Mask black - pale grey over forehead
above & under eye.

Wattles blue — cobalt

North Island Kokako   *Callaeas cinerea wilsoni*

When New Zealand's native forests started falling to the axes of European colonists, the North Island kokako population began to decline, and continues to do so. During the 1980s some birds were rescued from forests which were being destroyed and were transferred to the safety of Little Barrier Island. The South Island kokako, which has orange wattles, may now exist in very low numbers only on Stewart Island.

100

Black legs and
feet. Red wattle
- smaller in
female

North Island
♀ Saddleback

North Island Saddleback *Philesturnus carunculatus rufusater*
Before the turn of the century, cats and rats had exterminated the North Island
saddleback from the mainland and Little Barrier, Great Barrier and Kapiti islands.
The once widespread bird survived only on Hen Island, off the north-eastern coast
of the North Island. Recent work by the Wildlife Service has resulted in birds being
safely established or re-established on eight protected islands, including Little Barrier.

102

Rifleman *Acanthisitta chloris*

The diminutive rifleman, so named for the similarity in colour between its plumage and the uniform of the British Rifle Brigade of the last century, is often not seen or heard by visitors to the forest. Its very small size and arboreal habits keep it safe from most predators and it is still found in forests in many parts of the mainland and on Little Barrier Island.

Kereru *Hemiphaga novaeseelandiae*

The kereru, the New Zealand pigeon, has the largest body, and, in proportion, the smallest head of all New Zealand's bush birds, yet its agility when flying through the forest is remarkable. It is an entirely vegetarian species, eating leaves, flowers and fruits, the last being its preferred food. Kereru has adapted well to live in areas of mixed native and introduced vegetation, but destruction of native forests and illegal hunting are a continuing threat to its survival in many areas.

Tui *Prosthemadera novaeseelandiae*
The tui is the bold, noisy flier and songster of the forest and, if nectar and fruits
are available, often appears in suburban gardens. With nesting habits that keep it
away from most predators and feeding habits that have allowed it to adapt to
introduced plants, the tui is surviving well. Although described as a honeyeater the
tui also spends time feeding on berries and gathers large numbers of insects to feed
its chicks.

Tui

display posture

Agitated agressive
wing fluttering

Tui territorial display.

109

Bellbird *Anthornis melanura*

Because it tends to nest in nooks and crannies close to the trunks of trees rather than high up on a branch, the bellbird is vulnerable to predation by rats and stoats. Early this century the widespread species was also severely affected by disease, particularly in northern New Zealand. As the female bellbird is not inclined to travel far from her natal area, the birds are slow to recolonise their former habitats. Like the tui, the bellbird is a honeyeater and also eats berries and insects. It often shares the same habitat with the tui but is less conspicuous despite, in some areas, being more numerous.

Shining Cuckoo *Chrysococcyx lucidus*

With its distinctive loud whistling song, the shining cuckoo is considered by some to be the herald of spring. It is a migratory species, arriving in New Zealand from about mid August for its breeding season from islands north-east of New Guinea. As with the long-tailed cuckoo, the female lays single eggs in the nests of other small birds, relying on them to incubate the eggs and rear the chicks. When the cuckoo chick hatches, it pushes out the hosts' eggs or young from the nest and remains to be reared alone by the foster parents. The favoured host of the shining cuckoo is the much smaller grey warbler (*Gerygone igata*), a permanent resident of native forest and shrubland.

— Shining Cuckoo —

Grey Warbler   *Gerygone igata*

Although a bird of the forest, the grey warbler has adapted well to man-modified areas and is now a familiar bird in large suburban gardens and parklands. It is usually most noticeable in spring when its rapid melodic trilling becomes more vigorous. In the breeding season (August-January) the warbler usually raises two broods, although sometimes the second brood may be lost as a consequence of the parasitic shining cuckoo laying one of its eggs in the warbler's nest. Usually the warbler's first brood is safe, being raised well before the arrival of the migratory cuckoos.

Below: A grey warbler foster parent feeding a shining cuckoo chick.

When bringing food to the nest the
Grey Warbler will often sing with
a bill full of caterpillars

Even in full song
the bill is only
slightly open!

113

North Island Brown Kiwi *Apteryx australis mantelli*
As a result of forest destruction and competition from possums for nest and roost
holes, the North Island brown kiwi continues to decline in number throughout its
natural range. In Northland, however, where possums have arrived only recently,
the brown kiwi is still present in good numbers. Brown kiwis did not occur naturally
on any offshore islands. Birds were transferred to possum-free Little Barrier Island
in 1919 and, despite the high numbers of cats there at that time, they thrived.

Brown Kiwi.

A Second Habitat Repaired — Codfish Island

The slow and unpredictable progress of early sailing ships resulted in the establishment of human settlements in some most unlikely places — such as small, far-flung Codfish Island, lying three kilometres off the west coast of Stewart Island. Codfish, now a reserve, is not an easy island to land a boat on at the best of times but the first European arrivals on the island in the 1840s — seal hunters — thought it was a suitable place to live. They cleared little of the land but, to supplement their diet, they brought from Stewart Island and released on Codfish a predatory bird that was to have a disastrous effect on the island's other avian species — the weka.

While the weka is a native bird of New Zealand it is not present naturally on any of the country's smaller islands. When wekas do get to these islands they eat the eggs and chicks of nesting seabirds, and the adults of small species. Petrels, for instance, have been exterminated in this way on some islands. On Codfish, wekas reduced the number of Cook's petrels from tens of thousands to just a few breeding pairs within 100 years and they may well have exterminated other species. For the sake of the island's remaining species, not particularly to make a future home for the kakapo, which co-exists with the weka in both Fiordland and Stewart Island, the wekas were removed from Codfish. Indeed, when the weka project was first proposed in 1976, the presence of kakapo on Stewart Island was not recognised.

Like the eradication of the cats from Little Barrier, the removal of the wekas from Codfish was a long and determined effort organised by the Wildlife Service and participated in by many people in the interests of conserving a little of New Zealand's natural heritage. The last weka on Codfish Island was killed in 1984 but sign of these birds is so hard to find that it was not until 1987 that Wildlife Service staff were confident that all birds had been removed.

The weka was not the only problem on Codfish, however. Possums had been introduced too. Some experts considered these marsupials to be present in low numbers and hence unlikely to be much of a threat. But even a small threat could have proved disastrous for the now very rare kakapo. Possums would surely compete for food, nest cavities and daytime roosting places and we know that they eat eggs and possibly small chicks too. Originally the plan

---

Exposed to winds and rough seas, Codfish Island is difficult to get to by boat. Today's quick and efficient helicopter travel allows conservation work in such remote places to be effective.

was to remove the possums and then transfer kakapo over a period of many years. It was soon realised, however, that for the safety of the kakapo at least some of the Stewart Island birds had to be transferred quickly but it was also realised that the methods needed to remove possums from Codfish would seriously endanger the transferred birds. So the eradication of possums was started immediately and by early 1987 they had all been removed from the island.

The forests of Codfish Island are now just as secure for kakapo as were the forests of Stewart Island before man brought European rats and cats. The island is large enough to have a true mainland forest away from the effects of the sea. Rimu, which may be the key to successful kakapo breeding on Stewart Island, grows there in sufficient abundance and all the other kinds of native trees that occur on Stewart Island are there too. Weather patterns are similar as well, so fruiting of the trees should be easily 'predicted' by kakapo.

While shifting a whole population of birds may seem a drastic step (it has been done before with black robins in the Chatham Islands), such action may be necessary for the survival of the kakapo of Stewart Island. If the birds stay on Stewart Island they will surely be eaten by cats. On Codfish they will have a chance to live and breed. All the food, shelter and nesting places which we think they need are there. They can survive, and to increase in number they just have to find where the right food trees are growing.

By mid winter in 1987 some kakapo had been transferred from Stewart Island to Codfish Island. The original aim was to take birds from the fringes of the Stewart Island colony and to continue protection of the remaining birds at least until the kakapo on Little Barrier or Codfish islands could prove their ability to breed there. Sadly, though, we now know that there are too few birds left on Stewart Island for that population to be divided, so work has begun to move all the birds.

Brushtail Possum   *Trichosurus vulpecula*
The brushtail possum was introduced to New Zealand from Australia early in the nineteenth century to establish a fur trade. It spread quickly and today it is common in forests throughout the country where, because of its largely herbivorous feeding habits, it causes considerable damage.

Cook's Petrel *Pterodroma cookii*

The Cook's petrel is a small migratory species that was once abundant on Codfish Island. After the introduction of wekas to the island, the numbers of this burrow-nesting species declined dramatically. Once the wekas were eradicated, the species began to recover. Only one other major Cook's petrel colony exists – on Little Barrier Island. After the breeding season – spring through summer – the birds migrate to the eastern central Pacific.

Opposite

Fernbird *Bowdleria punctata*

Being inconspicuously coloured and a reluctant flier, the fernbird is more commonly heard than seen in its characteristic wetland habitat where it feeds on insects. It is not, however, an abundant species, owing to the drainage of wetlands for agriculture. Few people realise that the bird's distinctive 'u-tic' call is created by both birds of a pair – one calling 'u' and the other rapidly following with the 'tic'. The Codfish Island fernbird differs only slightly in plumage colouring from the subspecies found on the mainland, yet it has its own scientific name – *wilsoni*.

Kaka *Nestor meridionalis*

While the kea is the parrot of the mountain tops and the kakapo is the ground parrot, the kaka is the parrot of the trees of the forest. It is often noisy and very visible and this may lead to the belief that the species is numerous. The kaka, however, has been seriously affected by forest destruction, which has depleted its supply of insects, fruits and seeds, and by the introduction of possums, which compete for nest sites.

Opposite: A kaka sits alongside a large epiphyte (*Collospermum hastatum*).

122

grey sides to face

brown cap

obvious pale ridge
of feathers at moustache.
Warm naples, chest & belly
Sienna/red brown tail &
darker umber wings
Strong down curved bill

Brown Creeper *Finschia novaeseelandiae*
The brown creeper is a common bird of some South Island forests and shrublands,
and one of the most abundant birds on Codfish Island. Just why it has never inhabited
the North Island is a mystery.

Fiordland Crested Penguin *Eudyptes pachyrhynchus*

The Fiordland crested penguin nests in small colonies around the coast of Fiordland and on Stewart and nearby islands. When ashore during daylight, in the breeding and moulting seasons, the birds remain under dense vegetation to avoid the ever-present sandflies.

Southern Blue Penguin *Eudyptula minor*

The southern blue penguin is the southernmost relative of this family of small penguins which may be found right around the coast of New Zealand where the birds hunt mainly small fish. Nests are located in burrows, crevices or under buildings; they are easily identified by the pungent odour of the chicks' excreta. When the birds nest under buildings, humans often complain about their raucous love songs.

Of the Future

The kakapo, a most unusual bird, which has evolved out onto a limb, perfectly adapted for life in prehistoric New Zealand, would be thriving throughout the country were it not for the interference of man. Now, with assistance from man, it can expect no better than two secure island homes — Little Barrier and Codfish. It will be a sad day if, with all the resources available to us in this modern age, we cannot cater for the kakapo's modest needs.

There are now just 50 kakapo known to remain in the whole world — five in Fiordland, 16 on Little Barrier and 29 in the process of being transferred from Stewart Island to Codfish Island. We hope that a few more may yet be found on Stewart Island.

To ensure that islands such as Little Barrier and Codfish remain safe havens for wildlife, man also has much to learn. We do not need to exploit these lands for brief gains of cash or leisure. We can cease to be careless about carrying rats and cats on boats. We can learn to care for the fellow inhabitants of the earth — they have as much right to survive as we do.

Kakapo can survive on these islands — on Little Barrier they do have to learn about a whole new range of food with which to feed their young, but this is not an unrealistic challenge for them, and on Codfish Island all the ingredients are there for birds to breed and live unharmed.